SUDDEN COLLAPSES
IN PUBLIC PLACES

SUDDEN
COLLAPSES
IN
PUBLIC
PLACES

ॐ

JULIA DARLING

PUBLICATIONS
2003

Published by Arc Publications
Nanholme Mill, Shaw Wood Road
Todmorden, Lancs OL14 6DA

Copyright © Julia Darling 2003

Design by Tony Ward
Printed by Antony Rowe Ltd.,
Eastbourne, E. Sussex

ISBN 1 900072 91 2

Acknowledgments:
The author wishes to thank Monica Cheale,
all her fellow students on the MA in Poetry
at the University of Newcastle upon Tyne,
Linda Anderson, Desmond Graham,
Jackie Kay, Bill Herbert, Linda France
and Jo Shapcott for inspiration
and constructive criticism.
Thanks also to the songwriter Maggie Thacker
and 'Turkish Bath'who set 'Virginia'
to music, and to her family Bev Robinson,
Scarlet and Florence Darling.

'Ancestry' appeared in *Sauce* (Bloodaxe Books, 1995)
and 'Convalescence' was written for Linda France,
and published by Diamond Twig in
Modern Goddess postcard series (1993).

Cover drawing:
Copyright © Emma Holliday 2003

The publishers acknowlege financial assistance
from the Arts Council of England, Yorkshire.

Editor, UK & Ireland: Jo Shapcott

*Dedicated to the staff and
other waiting patients at the
Northern Centre for
Cancer Treatment.*

CONTENTS

HIGH MAINTENANCE

I am walking down a corridor
in the department
for the maintenance
of badly constructed
women.

We have medieval hips
We need scaffolding
We subside.

I have no arches, and my feet
land flat on the wormy floor.
You can hear me coming.
My sockets need rewiring,
there is damp in my wings,
fungi in my joints.

The department is a mess.
There are artificial limbs,
glass eyes, adhesive smiles
piled up. I can spend days
looking for a part.

'It's archaic here,'
I say to sweaty
Janet, who searches
in the broom cupboard
for her lost womb.

I bring in flowers,
pot pourri, room freshener,
presents for the crumpled clerks.
But there is always that smell
of knotted pipes, loose drains
sickness notes.

I must look hopefully at
the new basin in the Ladies.
And if I sing,
and wear ear plugs,
I never hear the word
demolition.

IMPERSONATION

because I have all day
I take time with
your NINETEEN PAGE FORM
in re-invented handwriting
I write a false name
an invented address
in an avenue
with a view
I find myself sniggering
HA HA this new woman
will unnerve the computer
startle the data base
she will have a doctor
with wings
she will have
no children
no history of diabetes
cancer or mental illness
or a single allergy
no pin number
no postcode
she will have no
category or shoe size
SHE DOESN'T WEAR SHOES
SHE IS A THOUSAND YEARS OLD
her existence will send a thrill
through the corridors
of marketing

like discovering
a Tasmanian tiger
in Northumberland Street
she is as untrodden
as a silky desert
unperturbed as new milk
she was born in a crack
between two millennia
here is my form
I'll tell the receptionist
my smile is a disentangled knot
there goes another one
she'll say, nibbling her nail
they give me the creeps
as if it was that easy
and she'll rip it to confetti
and hand me another
start again properly
Mrs Darling she'll snap
forms aren't funny

A COMFORTING CAR PARK

After the clinic I walk the back way
through the half built wastelands of the hospital
which is riddled with pipes and diggers
and temporary walkways, and rooms ripped
from other rooms, then re-stitched to walls,
ruptured corridors, leading to rubble
and portacabins, crooked signs that point
to ear nose and throat, to amputations
and the Chapel of Rest.

I cut through a car park, into a memory
of outings with my father, to other car parks;
we were going to a tea shop, somewhere
like Petersfield, in the blue Morris Traveller.
He always took us to tea shops, to order cakes.
He didn't make us walk. He hated exercise.
We ate teacakes and jam, got back into the car,
and drove home. Sunned seats warming our legs.

A WAITING ROOM IN AUGUST

We've made an art of it.
Our skin waits like a drum,
hands folded, unopened.
Eyes are low watt light bulbs

in unused rooms.
Our shoulders cook slowly
in dusky rays of light.
This morning we polished

our shoes, so that they should wait
smartly. Our wigs lie patiently
on our dignified heads.
Our mouths are ironed.

Acute ears listen for
the call of our names
across the room of
green chairs and walls.

Our names, those dear consonants
and syllables, that welcomed us
when we began,
before we learnt to wait.

Call us to the double doors
where the busy nurses go!
Haven't we waited long enough?
Haven't we waited beautifully?

TOO HEAVY

Dear Doctor,
I am writing to complain about these words
you have given me, that I carry in my bag
lymphatic, nodal, progressive, metastatic

They must be made of lead. I haul them everywhere.
I've cricked my neck, I'm bent
with the weight of them
palliative, metabolic, recurrent.

And when I get them out and put them on the table
they tick like bombs and overpower my own
sweet tasting words
orange, bus, coffee, June

I've been leaving them
crumpled up in pedal bins
where they fester and complain.
diamorphine, biopsy, inflammatory

And then you say
Where are your words Mrs Patient?
What have you done with your words?

Or worse, you give me that dewy look
Poor Mrs Patient has lost all her words, but shush,
don't upset her. I've got spares in the files.
Thank god for files.

So I was wondering,
Dear Doctor, if I could have
a locker,
my own locker
with a key.
I could collect them
one at a time,
and lay them on a plate
morphine-based, diagnostically,

with a garnish of
lollypop, monkey, lip.

THINGS THAT SHOULD NEVER HAVE HAPPENED

I should never have eaten avocado
or pizza. I should have stayed with pies,

cabbage, neaps. And why did I
travel to Spain and Morocco?

I should have remained on this island
drinking beer, not wine. I should not

have navigated tunnels and crossed bridges.
I was better off in a home made boat

in a small harbour, catching crabs,
boarding insignificant trains, using Tippex.

Carrier bags have not improved my life
neither has gourmet cat food.

And I could have done without the menopause,
motorway service stations, nylon tights,

long corridors, imitation fires, imported apples.
And the past. I could have done without the past.

SATSUMAS

She is gliding out of Marks and Spencers,
carrying a clematis, a pound of satsumas.
It's just after five. Her legs are heavy.

There is the bus station, green wrought iron,
a woman in blue, selling the Big Issue,
a long coated man with a face like a lion.

She sees the stone angel that flies from a column.
And a child is laughing, a bell is ringing;
the bones of the city breath in a rhythm.

The starlings gather. She peels a satsuma
seeing a bank that was once a tea room,
before that a hairdresser, before that a lane.

She is bulging with maps, with lost streets,
threaded through her like silver. Stone faces
look from the cornices. Perhaps she is turning

into stone? *It's alright*, she says out loud
to the closing shops. *I'm still here. Actually*
dropping her bag of satsumas

watching them fall onto the tarmac, rolling
bright and orange, against the grey.
Living fruit and stone. The kernel of things.

INSOMNIA

Sleep is a friend I have fallen out with,
I wish she would come back to me.

I bring her Valerian, milk and honey,
I plead with her, I promise her dreams.

I wander the house listening for her voice
lisping in the cupboards, beyond the walls.

She has sent me here, it's not the same
as the world by day. I have no friends.

I am alone in slumbering rooms
with snoring chairs and bare faced clocks

I used to love her velvet arms,
her fur kisses, her soundless caves.

If only she would tell me what I'd done
and what it is she wants from me.

HEALER

For my healer shall wear pink cardigans,
and she will be called Doris.

And she will live in a bungalow
near New York, which is in Tyne and Wear.

The bungalow shall be placed in the middle
of a windy green field, where cow parsley grows.

And she shall be elderly, and soft,
her wrinkles like mountain streams.

She shall never mention chakras or meridians
and neither will she play whale music.

Rather she will read the Daily Mail
and have poofees and paintings of dogs.

And she will place her eiderdown hands
on my forehead on Wednesday afternoons.

I will close my eyes and hear marching songs
and I shall fear no evil. Even though I walk

through the valley of death.

SQUARE DANCING

I found this square
and in it was my life.
Like a puzzle it divided
different ways,

two triangles or
infinite smaller squares.
There was my corner as a wife,
a deep red square

for all that wine I drank,
rectangular houses, cubes of pain,
the squares in which I reared daughters,
that oblong love affair.

In my spare time I cut it out
and stitched it to other squares:
a piece of sky; some matted earth
or thrown-out lives I found in Cancer Care.

If you look squares are everywhere.
I made a kind of soggy quilt.
I lie beneath it in my room
and spill out beyond the geometric hem.

WAITING ROOM

I'm waiting for
the drugs to work,
this rain to stop, for results,
the tea to brew
paint to dry,

for it to harden, to wear off
my hair to grow, morning,
the weekend, a miracle,
to be put through:

I'm waiting for a ship
to sail up Dean Street.

The right time,
my children to grow up,
for the posse to come over that hill,
I'm waiting for the sequel,
and I want to see who wins.

And I'm waiting for
a velvet curtain to rise,
the trumpets, the big drum,
the whole shebang,
a voice from centre stage

calling
over here
this way
it's your turn
now.

DON'T WORRY

about the food you haven't bought,
if your daughter caught that train,
the bill that came, the twinge
in your right leg. Don't fuss.
The washing on the line
will dry again. It's not your fault
So what if you lied?
Don't be ashamed.

And don't worry that you promised.
It doesn't matter about those promises. Let them go.
Just tell her you don't like her if you don't.
You needn't see the doctor with bad breath.
Behave badly. Lie on the floor.
Throw a tantrum if you're bored.
Be late. Be sordid. Eat six pies.
Or trick them by being euphoric.

Above your head a flock of geese
are flying South. Beneath your feet
worms aren't worrying.

LIVING IN THE NEW EXTENSION

First there were plaster bones, pushing through walls
that weren't there before. Sensations like
whirlpools in the lower cellars, a murder of crows

nesting in the parlour. The window frames cracked,
then subsidence; a shifting of deeper foundations
and the drains smelt of another century.

Then, what was once my home was given over
to a team of doctor gardeners, to phantom nurses.
So, I am living in a temporary extension

around the back. It's not what I'm accustomed to,
this quiet, glassy space. A couch. A chair. At night
when they've gone home, with their stethoscopes

and pesticides, I like to wander naked through
the ruined rooms, to smoke, and gaze at all that
space. Recall the wealth I once possessed.

WATER POWER

After visiting Cragside Gardens

I'm harnessing the power of water
like Lord Armstrong, who thought
in a gush of clarity, that water
could make light, and that dim rooms
might be illuminated. So,
I'm imagining light bulbs,
irrigation ditches, and pumps.

I'm opening channels within myself
letting waves swell and break.
It's still primitive. I am conducting
this experiment within a flimsy body.
Conditions are not ideal.
Sometimes all I get is sweat.
But some nights

I'm like Blackpool glowing,
a beacon to myself,
riding in a chariot made of light.
I've got the reins, a torch between my teeth,
slicing at darkness with a blade
riding the current. Some nights I can almost see
beyond, to where the path bends.

VANITY

One day my hairdresser will be an old woman,
her hands leathery from grease, her teeth yellow.

Will I notice as I too shall be old and battered?
Will I still totter to her salon above the travel agents?

Will we strain to see each other in the misted glass?
Shall we still speak hopefully of shape and style?

Or will we be wordless, knowing that the usual
will do? That I'm there to feel the wash

of warm water down my neck, the stroke of fingers,
to be snipped and tidied like a pensioner's garden?

When will it end, this preening and spraying?
This holding the mirror to the back of my head?

DENTAL ATTENTION

In the street of sweets, tangerines and saris,
Mr Mamouji meets my teeth.

He peeks inside as if he's greeting
a room of cautious refugees.

He suggests slow tweaks,
the removal of ancient mercury.

And talks of roots and my teeth fall
at Mr Mamouji's tactful feet.

They'll be a whitening soon,
a crowning of the feeble ones.

I heard them last night speaking
about him   the relief

of finding a man who understands
their need to come out of the dark.

WHERE THE LIVING MEET THE DEAD

As it begins to vaguely rain
the narrow lane becomes a track.

I drive on up, until
I reach a man-size hut.

Inside there's a ticket seller
in a blue peaked cap who

sells me an inexpensive ticket
to walk amongst the ruins

where, the guide book says
the living meet the dead.

I thank him as he lights a cigarette
and watches, unemotionally tanned.

I amble round the overgrown
stones, laced with forget me not and fern

until I find, as I have read,
the door into an underground chamber

where the guide books says
the living meet the dead.

I go inside. There is no light, but then
I see a rustling shape, trembling white:

an American tourist in a mackintosh
sheltering.   Thinking I am come.

THINGS I HAVE LOST

I lost my innocence first,
left it up a tree.
Kept seeing it caught there,
like a balloon,
too high to reach,
too full of air.

Then I lost IT.
IT was the map
you need to get
from room to room.
I lost IT big.

When my education
got mislaid,
I found work
in a laundry
full of white sheets.
I took them home
played at escape,
death and ghosts.

You can do a lot with sheets.

After that
I searched
and searched
for maturity

which I found
at the bottom
of my mother's
blanket box.

It's tartan.
I put it on my knees.
At nights;
I watch the news.

By day
I wrap it round my head
and hum,
not harming anyone.

THE BOY'S ROOM

I was tired of my guests
so I wandered upstairs,
found a locked door
at the top of my house
that wasn't there before.

Behind the door there was a room,
rather like a warehouse
full of retro stuff: juke boxes,
fifties mirrors, cocktail shakers
and lampshades.

The guests followed me,
oohing and aaahing,
envying my luck,
touching my things.

Then there was another door
with crooked wooden steps
leading upwards

I went alone and found
a boy's room, with a boy's
duvet cover and boy's mess
and an untidy wind
blowing through it.

I shouted down at the others
Come and see!
But no one heard
and I felt as if my
head was bursting with ghosts.

I couldn't breathe.

I ran back down.
Come with me to the boy's room,
I implored my guests.
I can't go there alone.

There is no boy's room, they said.
Just this lovely retro furniture.
So desirable. So chic.

MACAROON

I come across rumours about myself
projected onto the walls of the city.
Pale insubstantial ghosts, wordless films,
smelling of damp books, cold as flowers.
I hardly recognise myself. I am bony as a saint,
the colour of tombs. Insubstantial too,
crouching in a bath chair with a nurse who has wings,
administering morphine with a delicate spoon.

I must rush to a department store to buy rouge.
I must never be pale. I smile fiercely. Run.
There are words I must not say: *pain* or *Macmillan*.

But where is the camera? Let me show you
how heartily I can eat a macaroon.

FACIAL

Carol smoothed and rubbed my putty skin
in a narrow room; her hot flannels
circled hollow eyes, she scooped up
sweet, bitter creams. With feather fingers
she massaged my brow, lifted the slack
below my chin. We listened to whales.

When she'd finished she suggested
some colour. So I lay there, eyes closed
while she slapped on foundation
red lips, rouge. And then she left me there,
replenished with a mask of health,
for hours, laid to anxious rest.

AFTERNOON FILMS

Pull me into your bakelite living rooms,
let me smell your leather car seats.

Dress me in a waist, light my cigarette,
curl my hair, paint my mouth, my lashes.

I will wear eau de cologne, have pointy breasts.
Give me a script. Let my eyes shine.

If you pour me a dash, I'll sip and not smudge.
Let me pace your rooms, and never sit down.

Monochrome never bleeds.
My god, I am tired of this sofa.

DOING THE CROSSWORD

A fragment, or a tiny piece of you.
Spectacles slipped down your nose, some tune

whispered from the Phillips radio.
Together we gazed at words, brooded

and scribbled in the margins of the news.
The fire fell to ash in the rumpled room.

A flame flared up: a word broke through.
You always got the clues. I'm not sure I do.

THE GROVE

Here is a dusted street in a city,
a fold in the valley, a crease of red brick
threading the bank, a necklace of houses,
strung along by a river, desirable, leafy.

Two girls whisper. Towels flap on lines,
an argument fragments across the vale.
I peer through the glass, down the wild gardens
and dogs look back sadly. Cats stare into ponds.

A child cries and drops a tin bucket.
A man calls his pigeons back to the huts.
Smoke curls from a bonfire, far away there's a siren.
Flowers shudder then close. Someone calls TEA.

When I go, you'll be alone by the window
in this tilting house hanging over the vale,
with the hawthorn, the pond, the rebellious garden,
the light in the evening that fills every room.

OUT OF HERE

I want to build a road
so I'm conversing
with my arteries,
emailing the keepers
of my marshy wastelands.

I want it straight
so I'm dealing with
the mad hill dwellers
who live on the banks
of my lymphatics.

I'm meeting rogue cells
at midnight
in the hot garden
of my heart.

And angel Alsatians are
barking at the vandals
who try to
impede construction.

I'm building a road
for a fast car
so I can drive
over that hill
out of here
out of here.

HOSPITAL GEOGRAPHY

In the bowels of this place
a puzzled goddess gazes, frowns
at maps and blueprints of the maze

of geriatrics, noses, ears,
cancers, fractures, x-rays, bums
brains and hearts, lungs and pipes

sluices, morgues and casualty
amputations, things replaced,
and the corridors that snake between

the limbs of this enormous thing
that coughs and vomits, bleeds and sleeps
and wails all night for peace.

She sits beneath this rattling mess
and frowns until her temples ache
pulls out her hair, tries to gauge

probabilities, against the odds
structurally, given every stress
of one harmonious breath.

WOODEN SPOON

Here is my grandmother's wooden spoon.
The same spoon that beat it's path
through childhood fairy cakes
to a fruity menopause.

Feel its stern handle.
Look into its cracked bowl.
There is power in that worn wood

to make cakes rise, to thicken cream
to make grown men silent.
This is a working spoon.

Daughter, take this spoon
into your kitchen and stir.

THE MILL

After staying in A. J. P. Taylor's Mill House, Yarmouth, Isle of Wight

The ferry brings me over the water
opening its iron mouth, letting me
walk back onto the island.

There are stones, then water,
a percussion of ropes and shackles.
Then the Mill, with its long corridors

leading to rooms
I no longer need to visit.
Here the broken bric-a-brac

will never be mended
and armchairs splay out
their horsehair secrets.

Each painting wonders
if it might be valuable
after all this time.

At night Canadian geese
plan their route across oceans
flapping and shrieking.

I sit on the bench,
looking at the simple lines
of the estuary. Children wave

from the silhouettes of boats.
There are footsteps
on the old railway line.

All my history
is simplified to this:
water, stone, flight.

TURKISH BATH

Been squatting in the steam
Been lying on the marble slab
Been hanging out with flesh

Been grunting, been slumping,
Been groaning and farting
Been sweating and lathering

Been grieving and oozing
Been wallowing in the deep tub
Been a jelly, been slack

Been showing my scars
Been with my underbelly
Been right inside my pores

Been scrubbed up, been towelled
Been powder puffed, been oiled
Been got ready, been got ready

VIRGINIA

I've got this friend. She's called Virginia.
I meet her in the seedy parts of rooms.
I disapprove of her; the way she hangs around.
But I can't say no. She needs me. I need her.

I carry her in the pockets of my coat.
I smell of her, of rust and tar and ash.
We're always on the look out for a place
where we can be alone, where we can talk.

I want her like I want to be in love.
There's the rolling, the licking, then the flame,
the thin curl of smoke, the wickedness
reminding me of when our love was hot.

But I deceive myself. She bores me stiff.
Virginia's dreary, sallow and a liar.
Her flaws are many. I can't take her home.
She holds me in her hand and won't let go.

She's a drain. I should give her the push.
My other friends don't understand
why I won't walk away, why I sit
on windy steps when I could be with them.

It's just we go back years. We've had good times.
She's like Judy Garland in the valium days
I can't forget how bright she was and slim.
If I abandon her, where will she go?

I know. She'll vanish in a rattling cough,
leaving nothing but a stub, a nauseous stink,
that some cleaner will briskly wipe away.
And I'll wonder why we carried on this long.

WARD THIRTY SIX

We are people soaked in onion skins,
arms tied to tubes, in our blue chairs.
The maroon nurse sighs beneath the clock.

The trolley comes, the voice of England
offers us Horlicks, sugar, biscuits.
We sip and chew. We place our limbs,

and slump and doze to the beat of drips.
I do the crossword, find new words,
for 'wreckage' and then 'rebirth.'

CHEMOTHERAPY

I did not imagine being bald
at forty four. I didn't have a plan.
Perhaps a scar or two from growing old,
hot flushes. I'd sit fluttering a fan.

But I am bald, and hardly ever walk
by day, I'm the invalid of these rooms,
stirring soups, awake in the half dark,
not answering the phone when it rings.

I never thought that life could get this small,
that I would care so much about a cup,
the taste of tea, the texture of a shawl,
and whether or not I should get up.

I'm not unhappy. I have learnt to drift
and sip. The smallest things are gifts.

SUDDEN COLLAPSES IN PUBLIC PLACES

like buildings, people can disintegrate
collapse in queues, or in a crowded street

causing mayhem, giving kids bad dreams
of awkward corpses, policemen, drops of blood

but I'm stood here, a miracle of bones
architecturally balanced in my boots

I feel each joint, each hinge and spinal link
jolting to the rhythm of my breath

aware of every tremor in my joists,
and yet I'm scared I haven't done enough

to be re-enforced and girded, Christ, I fear
those flowers tied to lamp posts, dread the crash

ANCESTRY

Have you ever seen my extraordinary feet?
They are waders, descended from flippers.
My little toe is related to a prehistoric mollusc.

My legs are Gothic pillars designed in Barnet
by Presbyterians, who sang Jerusalem.
These columns could support cathedrals.

My womb is a wartime nurse,
functional, regular, robust.
A womb that purses its lips.

My belly is the pillow that old ladies die on.
It's Victorian linen, the best in the high street.
It clasps my insides with invisible dams.

My breasts are Scottish, from a line of sepia aunts
who wrapped their Bristols tightly in sealy cloths,
with nipples as distant as Iona.

Unfortunately my shoulders are related
to sorry uncles, they hunch and apologise,
sag and wait sadly for sympathetic arms.

But these fine ears are sisters of the sails
that carried cargoes off the flat sea.
They are adventurous and foolhardy.

And this face, that berates me at the hairdresser
and winces in bar mirrors is mine.
I moulded it from ancestral clay.

All mine, with its thumb prints
and crevices. It's not finished.
You can have it when I'm done.

CONVALESCENCE

First you must find a view,
then make a quilt of get well cards
and good wishes. Then unravel yourself,

each knot and tangle, crease and fist.
Undo them. Listen to each limb and crevice,
the voices of your bones,

chart the weather of your body,
the nuances of each breath.
Eat the food of your childhood,

Haliborange and small fingers of bread.
Wear dirty slippers. Forget about words
and pay particular attention to trees.

Be wary of animals and children.
Play Gregorian chants. No mirrors.
Do not wash. Watch insects.

Let things roll under the bed.
Do not plan. Remove all diaries
Be weak. Be languid.

Flow back into yourself
slowly, tentatively,
when the dust has settled

on the windowsill,
and you have quite forgotten
the colour of work.

END

Eventually, I was placed on a bed like a boat
in an empty room with sky filled windows,
with azure blue pillows, the leopard-like quilt.

It was English tea time, with the kind of light
that electrifies the ordinary. It had just stopped raining.
Beads of water on glass glittered like secrets.

In another room they were baking, mulling wine.
I was warm with cloves, melting butter, demerara,
and wearing your pyjamas. My felt slippers

waited on the floor. Then the door opened
soundlessly, and I climbed out of bed.
It was like slipping onto the back of a horse,

and the room folded in, like a pop up story
then the house, and the Vale. Even the songs
and prayers tidied themselves into grooves

and the impossible hospital lay down its chimneys
its sluices, tired doctors, and waiting room chairs.
And I came here.   It was easy to leave.

ABOUT THE AUTHOR

Julia Darling has lived in the North East since 1980 and began her writing career as a poet, working with a performance group *The Poetry Virgins* for many years, 'taking poetry to the places that least expected it'.

In 1995, she published a book of short stories, *Bloodlines* with Panurge Press, and many of these stories were broadcast on BBC Radio 4. She continues to write short stories, many of which are anthologised or broadcast.

In 1998, her first novel *Crocodile Soup* was published by Anchor at Transworld. The novel went on to be published in Canada, Australia, Europe and the United States and was long-listed for the Orange Prize. Her most recent novel, *The Taxi Driver's Daughter*, is published by Penguin.

Julia Darling has written extensively for the stage, her most recent works being *Attachments* (part of *Double Lives*) and *The Last Post* for Live Theatre in Newcastle upon Tyne, *The Black Path* for BBC Radio 3 (with the poet Sean O'Brien) and *Doughnuts Like Fanny's*, a play about Fanny Cradock, for Quondam Arts Trust.

She has worked on a number of arts and health projects, including work with elderly people in residential homes for Equal Arts, and running drama workshops for doctors and patients with the project

'Operating Theatre.' She is also running workshops in the University of Newcastle's English School on the use of poetry and creative writing in medicine, funded by the Royal Literary Fund.

In March 2003, Julia Darling became the second winner of the acclaimed Northern Rock Foundation Writer's Award, the largest annual literary award in England.